For Eli, Colette, and Eden.
May you always talk with God.

L.W.

"God is near, and accessible to us through prayer; what a needed reminder for all of us, young and old alike!"
RUTH CHOU SIMONS, Founder of gracelaced.com and Author of *Beholding and Becoming*

"Here is a wonderful way to teach children that they can talk to God when they are happy or sad, in need of help or in need of forgiveness. It's a beautiful book with a needed message."
MELISSA KRUGER, Director of Women's Initiatives for The Gospel Coalition

"For kids and adults, sometimes prayer can feel intimidating. What do I say? Does God really care about that? This book shows just how simple it is to talk with God because of what Jesus has done."
J.T. ENGLISH, Lead Pastor, Storyline Fellowship, Arvada, Colorado, and Author of *Deep Discipleship*

"I can't think of a more perfect way to teach about prayer and the practice of approaching God. This will be a staple in our discipleship routine!"
PHYLICIA MASONHEIMER, Author, Founder of Every Woman a Theologian, and Host of Verity Podcast

"Prayer is hard for our children—they can't see who they are speaking to. Over and over again I am asked, 'How can I help my children to pray?' Start here!"
ED DREW, Founder of Faith In Kids and Author of *Meals With Jesus*

"This book will help our kids have a BIG view of God and see the incredible gift he has given us in prayer. Then they can spend their lives loving him and loving others, and the world will change."
JENNIE ALLEN, NYT Bestselling Author of *Get Out of Your Head* and Founder of IF:Gathering

"This beautifully illustrated book gives a 'through the whole Bible' picture of prayer, including a brilliant look at how Jesus prayed. It's really inspiring."
VICTORIA BEECH, Creator of GodVenture

"Encourages and empowers every child to know that there is nothing too small or too big to share with God."
RACHEL TURNER, Founder of Parenting For Faith

"A beautifully written and illustrated book with a simple message but chock-full of gospel and theology."
KRISTIE ANYABWILE, Author, Speaker, and Founding Member of The Pelican Project

"Laura Wifler understands that simple, deep truths shape and change lives. This is a book that will, by God's grace, lay the foundation for a thankful, praying life in lots of little lives."
COLIN BUCHANAN, Musician

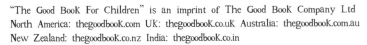

Any Time, Any Place, Any Prayer
© The Good Book Company / Laura Wifler / Catalina Echeverri 2021.

Illustrated by Catalina Echeverri | Design & Art Direction by André Parker

"The Good Book For Children" is an imprint of The Good Book Company Ltd
North America: thegoodbook.com UK: thegoodbook.co.uk Australia: thegoodbook.com.au
New Zealand: thegoodbook.co.nz India: thegoodbook.co.in

Published in association with the literary agency of Wolgemuth & Associates, Inc.

ISBN: 9781784986605 | Printed in Turkey

written by: LAURA WIFLER   illustrated by: CATALINA ECHEVERRI

ANY TIME
ANY PLACE
ANY PRAYER

Many years ago — nearly
as long ago as you can
go — two people lived with
God in a beautiful garden.

They were Adam and Eve, and
they were friends with God.

They could talk with him
about every thought they had.

Every question they wondered.
Every feeling they felt.

They told him
anything, anytime.

But one day, the devil
slithered into the garden
as a snake.

He spoke to Eve
and suggested that
God did not love
her and Adam.

Adam and Eve
decided that the snake's
words sounded better than
God's words...

so they chose not to trust and obey
God anymore. This is called sin —
and sin spoils beautiful things.

Now, Adam and Eve were
afraid of God.

The next time God came to
talk with them, they hid.

But God found them. He told them that
because of their sin, they would have to live
outside God's garden, separated from him.

Now people couldn't be with God.
But they could still talk with him.

Talking with God is
called "prayer."

But because of sin, prayer
was sometimes hard.

Sometimes people didn't
Know what to pray to God.

Sometimes they didn't
want to pray to him.

And sometimes, they
were just plain ol'
scaredy pants.

The Law

The Prophets

The Words of Wisdom

But God kept reminding his people that he wanted them to talk with him about anything, anytime, anyplace.

So they prayed...

Miriam (Exodus 15)

When they felt their love for God so much they thought their hearts might burst!

Hannah (1 Samuel 1)

When they wanted something so badly it was all they could think about.

When they knew they had sinned and needed forgiveness.

Jonah (Jonah 2)

Nehemiah (Nehemiah 6)

When they needed help to do the right thing.

God's people
prayed many times — millions
and billions of times — until one
day, God the Father sent his
Son, Jesus, to earth.

Jesus invited people to be his friends.

Because he was God, talking with him was like being back in the garden! It was awesome!

And because Jesus was a man, he understood his friends' feelings and their questions about living in a world spoiled by sin.

Yet Jesus was different from other people. He didn't ever sin — he always loved and obeyed his Father.

Jesus talked with his Father –
any time, any place, any prayer.

He told God how he felt...
what he needed...

and what he
was thinking.

And he helped his friends know
how to talk with God too:

"Our Father in heaven,
your name be honored as holy.
Your Kingdom come.
Your will be done
on earth as it is in heaven.
Give us today our daily bread.
And forgive us our debts,
as we also have forgiven our debtors.
And do not bring us into temptation,
but deliver us from the evil one."

One day, Jesus told his friends that he had to leave
this world. They begged him not to go.

Jesus told them not to be afraid. Jesus promised to send God's Spirit to come and live in them, so they could be closer to God than ever!

The Spirit would be with them ALL OF THE TIME, everywhere they went. Basically, things would be MORE AWESOME!

But first Jesus had to
die on the cross. Because
everyone sins, everyone
deserves to pay the cost
of sin, which is to be
separated from God forever.

Instead, through his death,
Jesus paid for our sins,

so that people could
be with God forever.

Jesus didn't stay dead.

His Father raised him back to life!

Jesus went back to heaven and sent his Spirit to his friends, just as he'd promised.

Now there was nothing stopping anyone
from being friends together with God!

Jesus' friends didn't ever have to
be afraid of talking with God...

Perpetua and Felicity (about 182-203)

about anything...

William Tyndale (1494-1536)

anytime...

Susanna Wesley (1669-1742)

anyplace.

John M. Perkins (1930-)

The Bible

God says that anyone who loves and trusts
Jesus as their friend and King can talk to him
like this. You can pray about anything.

You can tell God every
thought you have.
Every question you wonder.
Every feeling you feel.

You can pray...

When you feel your
love for God so much
you think your heart
might burst!

God, you are AMAZING!

When you want something so badly it's all you can think about.

When you sin and need forgiveness.

When you need help to do the right thing.

You can pray...

For a friend
who is sick.

After a dream
you had.

To say thank you
for your food.

About adventures
you want to go on.

About what to do with
your new ninja moves.

Most of all, you can pray
for God's help to love the
things he loves and obey
the things he says.

And if you're really sad or things are really bad, and all you feel like you can do is groan and say...

EURRREEEOOGH

the Spirit will know exactly what you need, and he will pray for you.

You can pray anytime, anyplace.

In the car.

In the morning.

At the playground.

In the nighttime.

In your
bedroom.

In your bathroom.

By yourself.

With your family.

With a friend.

Someday, Jesus will return, and his friends will live with God in his perfect and beautiful world – FOREVER!

We'll talk with God face to face, just like in the garden.

Until then, we can talk
with God — any time,
any place, any prayer.

Why not do it right now?

HOW DO WE KNOW ABOUT
TALKING WITH GOD ANY TIME, ANY PLACE, ANY PRAYER?

This storybook opens with God, the beginning of the world, and the first two people to ever pray. In Genesis 1 – 2 we see how easy it was to talk with God. But in chapter 3, Satan caused Adam and Eve to doubt and disbelieve God's promises. Ever since, prayer has often been hard, scary, or unimportant for God's people. Yet God always made a way for his people to talk with him through prayer. In Exodus 15, Miriam expresses her joy. In 1 Samuel 1, Hannah shares her sorrows. In Jonah 2, Jonah confesses his disobedience. And in Nehemiah 6, Nehemiah asks for help.

In the Gospels, we see Jesus modeling how to talk with God. In Matthew 6, Jesus specifically teaches us how to pray through the Lord's Prayer. When Jesus returned to heaven, he sent his Holy Spirit to live inside his people (Acts 2:1-4). One of the roles of the Spirit is to help God's people see how prayer is always possible, wonderful, and important. Someday God will live with his people again (Revelation 21:3), and then we'll enjoy talking with him face to face—just like Adam and Eve did at the beginning of the world.